How To Be Married To 2 Men

Yushonda Tarver

Copyright © 2019 by **Yushonda Tarver**

All rights reserved. No part of this publication may be reproduced by any means, graphics, electronic, or mechanical, including photocopying, recording, taping, or by any information storage retrieval system without the written permission of the publisher except in the case of brief quotations embodied in critical articles and reviews.

Yushonda Tarver/Rejoice Essential Publishing
PO BOX 512
Effingham, SC 29541
www.republishing.org

Unless otherwise indicated, scripture is taken from the King James Version.

"Scripture quotations taken from the Amplified® Bible (AMP), Copyright © 2015 by The Lockman Foundation. Used by permission. www.Lockman.org"

How To Be Married To 2 Men/ Yushonda Tarver

ISBN-13: 978-1-946756-85-5

LCCN: 2019919097

Table of Contents

INTRODUCTION...1

CHAPTER 1:   Love, Lust, Life.................3

CHAPTER 2:   The Real Makeover..........16

CHAPTER 3:   The W's in Wife..............22

CHAPTER 4:   Do Marriages Fail or Do People Fail Marriage?........................33

CHAPTER 5:   Vision Versus Vision......42

CHAPTER 6:   Advantage Versus Disadvantage......50

CHAPTER 7:   Whose Identity Are You Married Into?..........55

CHAPTER 8:   Whose Wearing The Secret Parachute In This Marriage?...........61

CHAPTER 9:	Knowing Your Man........64
CHAPTER 10:	Who's Idea Was This?...............................74
CHAPTER 11:	The World's Way Or Your Way?.................78

ABOUT THE AUTHOR....................................85

Introduction

What qualifies my marriage out of so many married and divorced couples to be a spokesperson on such a topic as how to be married to a man, especially when no two people or their marriages are the same? People have all types of reasons for getting married. Everyone, for the most part, thinks they have found 'the one'. 'My soulmate' is what most call that special one. Well, this is a little different. This isn't love at first sight or pent-up desire for another. I'm not saying that those feelings don't matter or mean anything at all those are normal human feelings.

Questions to consider:
1. Whose idea was it to constitute marriage?
2. What is the real meaning of marriage covenant?
3. What is the purpose of marriage?
4. Did you hear anything about the person that you would like to marry or have already married?

Are these legitimate questions to know the answer to or does it matter as long as your feelings are being gratified? Well, if someone left a note on your door without a name, wouldn't you like to know who the note was from? If someone hit your car, would you like to know if they were insured? If you become pregnant, would you like a sign that you are pregnant besides spontaneous labor? How much more should one understand the covenant within the constitution of marriage? You know, most people don't start asking questions until it's time to be responsible for someone or something or the favorite hitter you hurt my feelings...

CHAPTER 1

Love, Lust, Life

WHICH IS THE REASON TO MARRIED:
LIFE, LOVE OR LUSt

Life

Life is such a broad topic. So many things can happen within one's life that can lead or pull them away from the very idea of marriage. Let's examine a few reasons that this might happen. Our parents or guardians told us that a good education was highly important, so we spent our first 12 or more years pursuing just that or not. Either way, education is put out there as important. In return, you hope for a good career or job that would keep you all the days of your life. See the thing about that is this one small fact that is so easy and yet misunderstood. Are you ready? **YOU DIDN'T CREATE YOURSELF!!** I know but it's true. We try things out just to find out that's not what we want. We go places just to find out that that's not what we had in mind. We try on things just to see that we don't look the way we thought we would in it. We taste things just to see if we like it and if not, spit it out.

All of these things we try out are fine in its place, but what happens when you have been training yourself for the perfect fit, the perfect taste, the perfect location, or the perfect career? We all have these experiences, for the most part, with ourselves in mind, not really paying much attention to our creator God and His fit for us. We come into this world, putting a demand on what we want and how fast we should get it. Self-centered is what it's called. I know that we don't want to be viewed as that, but it's true. These few things can make or break us.

Lust

Lust is a very strong word, so let's make sure we keep it in content and context. Lust from the Father's perspective is this craving for sensual gratification. We look for those things or people that will meet our instant gratifications on a regular basis, if possible, and if not through someone, then through something. We never know that this way never works in a union such as marriage. What happens when you have a strong desire for something? How have you pursued it? What did it cost you and were you willing to pay the price? Was it worth it? Sometimes we don't look at our desires as lust, but if what you are chasing after of is of this world, then its lust and this way will lead to the destruction of the mind and soul. This will also cause marriages to be destroyed if you have this type of mindset.

Love

Let's look at our last one: love. Now when we speak about love, we have to be mindful that love and lust runs along a very thin line and if you are not mindful, you will be saying one and acting out the other. This is highly toxic to oneself and the other person you are wanting to join yourself to. Whose idea of love are we acting out? Is it our parents? Is it our imaginations? Is it something that we see out in the world and said, "This must be love and I want it." Just because we have a strong liking for someone doesn't make it love. Just because you can't see yourself without that person doesn't make it love. Let's look at the Father's definition of love.

1 Corinthians 13:4-5 (AMPC), "Love endures long and is patient and kind; love is never being envious nor boils over with jealousy; is boastful or vainglorious, does not display itself haughtily 5 is not conceited (arrogant and inflated with pride) it is not rude (unmannerly) and does not act unbecomingly. Love (God's love in us) does not insist on its own rights or its own way, for it is not self-seeking; it is not touchy or fretful or resentful; it takes no account of the evil done to it (it pays no attention to a suffered wrong)."

See the difference in our definition of love and the Father's? I have come to have a greater respect for the Father's understanding than my own. Just because I thought one thing to be something doesn't change the fact that it isn't. It is the Father's good pleasure to give us His children the kingdom. And allow me to drop this on you: you can't have his ways and benefits without him. It is Father God that can separate the world from the Kingdom. We want Kingdom marriages, not worldly ones.

When joining oneself to such an institute as marriage, you might try doing a little research. The three words above alone will keep such a union as marriage good when in their rightful place, but it's just not enough. It's going to take all of heaven to help you become what Father God had in mind for His union called marriage. Here in the word, Father God tells us the heart of the Father is to bring you and your spouse together.

Malachi 2:15 (AMPC), "And did not God make (You and your wife) One (flesh)? Did not one make you and preserve your spirit alive?

And why did God make you two One? Because He sought a godly offspring [from your union]. Therefore, take heed to yourselves, and let no one deal treacherously and be faithless to the wife of his youth.

Here is vision at its best. Take notes and learn from the Father. Don't leave him out of His own plans for your life, daughters. Let's not act as rebellious teens who can't wait to get from under a covering that we think of as controlling. I call it a controlled environment where we are safe to grow and make mistakes and no one takes advantage of us. It's where we receive our counsel and we ask our questions. It's where we are healing from the heartbreaks of our upbringing and the imprints of our souls.

Father has a plan for us, Daughters of Zion. Let's no longer seek out ungodly ways to be wives. We can still be strong God-fearing women. We can still give our body's in marriage and yet maintain our chasteness before Father God. Ladies, I know some of you probably didn't grow up with your dad. I sure didn't grow up with mine, so I know firsthand what it's like not having one or to be mindful of a father and his thoughts on what you should and shouldn't do. I know for the most part, whether you had your dad or not, dads hold this image of a brick wall, plus the US military, plus all of his illegal threats that he just might make good on if given the chance, which spells out no life or fun because you are daddy's little girl. Some dads messed up that image by not being there or some dads died at whatever age. Some dads were mean and abusive, some are in prison, or maybe you are a product of rape or incest. Whatever the reason, it does not, or ever can, change the fact that you first belonged to your Heavenly Father and He has always had a plane for your life. So maybe your dad was there, maybe not, but let's not willfully leave out Father God for He cares and loves us so much.

Now, let's be real. There are several ways to prepare oneself for a husband. Let's look at them closely and see if you see yourself in any of the examples. It's okay to self- examine. You might find out some things about yourself that have been tucked away for so long and asking to be dealt with.

NINE POSSIBLE REASONS

1. Mother and Father teaching you and telling you that you will one day be a wife.
2. Life starts happening to you, and you meet someone at a young age. You're in love, and you want to be together forever.
3. You meet a really nice guy and you don't want anyone else to have him.
4. You are tired of being alone/single.
5. You would like to start a family and you are getting no younger.
6. All your friends are getting married and if you go to one more wedding...!
7. You think that all women should be married.
8. You want to have a long life sex partner and not be looked upon as a whore.
9. You find out you are pregnant.

And the list could really go on. Whichever one it is for You, it will not change the rules to how it's done, especially if you are going to be successful at it.

I remember as a little girl, around eight years old, I was walking up the hallway of my grandmother's house and I just stopped and said that I wanted to have a husband and two boys. Wow! What a prayer. You will find out why I say that later. Growing up, I really didn't see great relationships or healthy relationships that made me say I want that kind of relationship. As a matter of fact, I said no way will a man treat me like what I saw the men around me treating the women they say they loved or had children with.

I grew up hearing and seeing the ongoing ill-treatment of women of all ages, financial backgrounds, and races. It was real!! I sometimes shared in the company of many of those women who told me about their on-going hurt and pain. Even then, at the age of eight, I had an understanding of their issues, meaning a word to comfort them.

So many women are stuck in the crossfire of their inner emotions and desire to be with a man that it almost kills them. Women find themselves giving more than they get in return. I want to share something at this very moment as I'm typing at my computer. My eyes are filling up with tears because I feel the deep pain and sorrow of you women that will read and share this book with other women. You have given and given and given till you are out: out of money, friends, family, house, car, food, ministry, life, and health. You have lost sight of YOU while trying to be the ONE! The one who he comes home to, the one who has his heart, the one he has sex with, the one he says I do to, the one he gives his freedom for, the one he tells his family and friends about, or the one he chooses over the rest. This is how we end up in this emotional roller coaster called love, but it's not love at all. It's so far from the truth. You just don't know the rules to the life you are trying to live, so you go about it the wrong way, getting dragged through the mud of life.

Now you want to give up and just have at it! You start making up your own rules. You surround yourself with people that have been hurt worse than you. Team what now! "We gone do it our way! Let's show them how to play this game," you say, and you start. It feels and looks good for a minute. As a matter of fact, you become the captain and spokesperson, not knowing you are telling the rest how to live more defeated in their emotions, money, wealth, decision making, families, ministries...Well, you get the point. No further than you were when you were 'team I'. You cannot keep company with silly women whose whole aim is to break themselves and others down at any cost! You become the company you keep – physically and spiritually. Somewhere you have to stop and ask, "What am I doing wrong?" and not just look for a better way to do more of what you are doing wrong.

THAT GET BACK SPIRIT

Getting back at someone for what they said or did to you is another form of self-abuse. Ninety-nine percent of the time, this type of abuse steams from our childhood/upbringing. What you do to me, I do worst to you! So, getting back at someone is practiced as a little girl and it rolls over into our adulthood relationships. Do you remember the first time someone hurt you when you were young and you did something mean to them and were told to say that you were sorry without the evidence of the other person changing or feeling sorry for what was done to you? See, the enemy of our soul works through our relationships to try and destroy us and take us off the path God would have us on. So already having a negative experience with mistreatment has left a mark on your heart. Depending on the person, reasons for making you say that you were sorry and them explaining their reason why to you will determine to be harmful or helpful as you become older.

Ladies, you haven't even made it to the altar yet. It's a good thing to be able to trace your issues back to its source instead of not knowing or saying it doesn't matter when clearly it does. I mean, you have carried these childhood issues all your life. Place them where they belong. Get an understanding of who, when, what, where, and, most of all, why.

We often shun away from the past because it hurts. You don't remember. It would really hurt people if it came out. You have a fear of the outcome. The person with the answer is now gone! There are so many reasons to want to forget, but now it's about being free to put this garbage in the trash once and for all and stop carrying this mess around. No more! We want a man to love us for who we are, and he doesn't even know that we are crazier than a bag of cat litter. And woo! Don't let it be generational. He's really in for it. That means your mother, mother, mother had the same issues. No, no, cut it off at its source. We are giving ourselves permission to be free and whole. We will no longer carry around false and unidentifiable perceptions of the women and men that raised and influenced us.

CHAPTER 2

The Real Make Over

Finding out that your covenant vows came with more than one person can be very challenging. We take vows in front of a judge, minister, family, and friends. Then we dance, have cake and go home or to our special detailed honeymoon, not knowing that you took covenant vows with an unseen third person.

We speak about it, we say it, but do we really get it. We ask him to help with getting that person to commit. We ask Him to help plan the wedding. We even say help with the budget. But when we get what we want, so many times we make Him stay at the altar and meet us back at the court-room for divorce. Ladies, it is highly pivotal that we understand where our help in marriage comes from. Yes, we have family, friends, girlfriends and yes, my favorite, IN-LAWS! Yes, all those people are good for their advice, but your marriage is uniquely custom fitted to both of you. The sooner you understand this, the better, for it will save you much time, pain and money.

IGNORANCE- lack of knowledge or information. I always say, "Ignorance isn't bliss when you're the rabbit in the foxhole."

See! It's in the knowing. I want to drive home this point: for Holy Spirit will guide and lead you in any and all areas of your life, but you have to invite Him in. He will not take over your life or marriage. Yes, the Holy Spirit is all-knowing, but He is not intrusive. I hope you are getting the big picture. Father God has given us His Holy Spirit to richly invest in us so we can actually get it right. This marriage life doesn't have to be complex at all, but it must be done His way.

Before I realized that the Holy Spirit was in my marriage, I would make emotional decisions. I had highs and lows like no other. If something went right, then I did well. I listened to what my granny taught me; I obeyed my family. If things went wrong, well, then it was your fault. You did not listen. You are so selfish. You don't care. You are so stupid. Well, I think by now you see the 'you and I relationship' of who gets the credit and who gets the blame. That way of doing things got me nowhere fast but more of what I didn't want. I was done with the line we quote to ourselves: "No one is perfect. This is just the way it is going to be."

Well, after a five-year journey, that wasn't working anymore because somewhere on the inside of me was saying I could have greater, more, and joy. Was this wishful thinking or was Father God showing me something that I had not seen Before? His plan and vision for me and my marriage is what He was trying to get to me. But somewhere along the line, I had to ask and want the help and be willing to do the work. I know we just want Jesus to take the wheel. "Make it right, Lord," we say. Never do we ask the Lord what He wants. We never ask Him, "How would you like to handle this situation for me?"

Proverbs 19:14 says, "House and wealth are an inheritance from fathers, but a prudent wife is from the LORD. "

The Bible clearly tells us where to find this type of woman. The Lord also lets man know that "A man that finds a wife finds a good thing and obtains favor from the Lord." See it's something special about us as women that only the Lord Himself can give such a woman as Proverbs 31. Anything else is a migraine. Ladies, we must allow the Lord to make us over.

I believed that because I heard the voice of God in regards to who my husband was, everything else would be perfect and I would live out my days in joy because I had my share of pain from a child. I didn't know Father God had a different kind of perfection and that would be to transform me into the image of His son Jesus Christ, and this would really hurt but for the good! He was about to begin surgery and all that I had been through was just pre-op. Getting me ready for the big chop - the big makeover.

See, we look so pretty on our wedding day but the 'not so pretty us' is ever-present with us, and the beauty treatment will begin stripping away at every layer of fabric, makeup, hairpieces, you name it. It will come off all in the name of destiny and purpose to perfect the woman He had in mind and what joy you would bring Him.

The pain the Father feels when we hurt and when we are rejected by others is real. All we have to know is He has been waiting with open arms to fix it all. He wants to whisper in our ear, "I love you, daughter! I have always been here! For I have always been here! I was there at your conception! I watched you grow in the darkness! I watched every toe and every finger go in the place that I set it! I watched as your hair grew and the color that it would turn into! I watched your skin change into just the right shade of color! Before you could even open your eyes, I knew their color! I see the height that you would be long before you would be measured! I knew you in your darkness! Now come to the light and get to know me, your Heavenly Father, the one who knew you before you were planted in the womb of your mother."

A worthy woman who can find her? Proverbs 31:10 (AMP) says, An excellent woman [one who is spiritual, capable, intelligent, and virtuous], who is he who can find her? Her value is more precious than jewels and her worth is far above rubies or pearls. "

It's time to show and prove that the Father has real women on His team, and we are worth our salt. So don't accept any more phone calls, dates, late-night pop-ups in the name of I can't sleep from thinking about you, no more face Face Timing from the neck down, no more snap chats, and no more bathroom selfies. Remember ladies, our Daddy God won't take to kind of His princess sharing herself with a thief because that's what he is if he tries it any other way. Go ask my Daddy God, for I know my worth!

CHAPTER 3

The W's In Wife

We practice what we hear and see! Practiced behavior becomes a lifestyle!

How often do we as women bring up something we heard or have seen as little girls or young teens as it relates to relationship issues? We have, for the most part, seen mistreatment or improper treatment from the men in our lives invade the hearts of the women who raised us unconsciously.

We have been carriers of the pain or joy we have witnessed. This form of unconsciousness in our thoughts and behaviors has been given space within our time, and for the most part, we claim it with honor without investigating the source of why it is that we do what we do.

We tell ourselves and others, "This is the way that I am. Take it or leave it," as if by some sort of knowing this about yourself brings glory and self-identification to your dysfunction. It's this type of behavior that leads to the downfall of our relationships. Let's start examining those family traditions that have been passed on from our Mother's and Father's houses and determine whether they make for our good. If it didn't work then, chances are it's not going to work now.

We cannot change how our parents reacted to each other, but we sure can control whether we act the same way or not. We must be willing to venture off into our subconscious mind and do a little probing because remember you think the way that you are, but sometimes you act the way you have seen. This brings to mind the passage in the word of God when Jesus states in the book of

St. John 5:19, So Jesus answered them by saying, "I assure you and most solemnly say to you, the Son can do nothing of Himself [of His own accord], unless it is something He sees the Father doing; for whatever things the Father does, the Son [in His turn] also does in the same way. So, it is very important how we see and hear and even more important who we see doing it.

Let's look into the 5 W's:

WHO ARE YOU?

This question is more important than you realize. If you are wanting to give your lifetime commitment to a man, then you better be sure about the answer. You need to be able to show and tell him just who you are and if you are unsure, then it is your responsibility to find out not his.

So many times, we as women put our personal power into a man to help us discover something in ourselves that we can't see. When a man looks at you, trust me, it's with himself in mind. You must never give up on the power of knowing you, because the day you do, you're dead. You have nothing to offer and having nothing to offer will lead to being dormant, bitter, and unsatisfied.

He is not your creator. Father God is, and if you have not gone to the Father for your personal blueprint, then a man will just turn you into the image he had in his mind when he first saw you.

WHAT ARE YOU?

This is another very important question to also know the answer to for several reasons. This is one of the W's that will bring you and your husband great joy or pain. All of your actions will get their legs from this W of what you count as truth your belief system, what you remember, what you care about, what you are willing to give or give up, and what you envision as a wife, mother, provider to your career. Knowing this will keep you sure-footed on the day of testing. Oh yes, you will be tested in this area big time!

The two shall become one flesh. What you bring to the table will be the meal you eat. Know what you are serving. It's said that 'the way to a man's heart, is through his stomach.' Yeah, if he's an animal. It will take more than a home-cooked meal to keep him happy. It's little folktales like this one that keep us thinking like silly little girls instead of grown women.

WHY?

Why you and not someone else? Your 'why' has to be very strong for it's in your 'why' that you will draw much strength. 'Why' settles the matters of the heart? How many times have you ask yourself why am I this way or another? Why did I do that? Why do I keep finding myself in these types of situations? Why won't he? Why want she? Why, why, why as the tears flow? The cry of 'why' can make or break you as well as all of your relationships. Did you not know that you become your inner 'why'?

WHERE?

Where do I see myself as a woman, wife, or mother? Where will these different positions take me? Will I remain me or will I lose myself? Will a husband be able to flow with where I see myself? I know where I'm going, but will this pathway take me there or derail me? All these questions are valid for the simple fact that you need to know the answer to all of the w's so that when life, distractions, events, setbacks, or disappointments confront you, you can find your way because you know where you are going. Never lose sight of who and where you are. You have an inner map quest GPS, better known as the Holy Spirit of God.

WHEN?

When is another taker because we as women want to rush things because of our inner emotional need for it. That feeling of, "I'm not getting any younger. When will it be my turn? I'm so fed up with waiting! Why is it taking so long?" I would say to that type of strong desire, "Wait," for you know not what it will take to carry what it is that you are so impatient about. Marriage is like being pregnant and preparing yourself mentally, physically, emotionally, financially, spiritually, but most of all, it's timing because you can have all that in place and miss your timing. Then it's back too square one — the disappointment in preparing just to miss your timing. That's what happens when we as women try and jump ahead of God without counseling with Him first.

Understanding the five w's is highly critical to your success in any relationship, especially when it comes down to Father God and His institution called marriage. The more you learn about the Lord Jesus and the relationship He has with the Father, the more you will come to know yourself in a greater way. The Holy Spirit will begin to show you things about yourself that you thought were impossible. I mean, who better to introduce you to your husband then the Creator Himself.

Don't steal that moment away from the Father by being impatient or thinking that it doesn't matter to Him and just marry anybody and work out the details along the way. No. He has feelings involved too. He has cared for you, watched you grow, and waited for you to come into the knowledge of Him and His eternal plan for your salvation, life, ministry, business, marriage, motherhood, and friendships. He wants to be there for you, but you have to wait for His season and timing through the chain of events, events that to you are unnecessary or issues, for it's through these types that He wills His perfect will. Let patience have her perfect work in you. It will bring about a great virtue like no other that you will need in this covenant union, that you are so longing to be in, called marriage.

The finished product in your W is the Proverbs 31 Woman. Your transformation looks good on you!!!

Proverbs 31 (Amplified Version)

WHO?

[10] An excellent woman [one who is spiritual, capable, intelligent, and virtuous], who is he who can find her? Her value is more precious than jewels and her worth is far above rubies or pearls.

[11] The heart of her husband trusts in her [with secure confidence], And he will have no lack of gain.

WHAT?

¹² She comforts, encourages, and does him only good and not evil All the days of her life.

¹³ She looks for wool and flax And works with willing hands in delight.

¹⁴ She is like the merchant ships [abounding with treasure]; She brings her [household's] food from far away.

WHEN?

¹⁵ She rises also while it is still night And gives food to her household And assigns tasks to her maids.

¹⁶ She considers a field before she buys or accepts it [expanding her business prudently]; With her profits she plants fruitful vines in her vineyard.

WHERE?

¹⁷ She equips herself with strength [spiritual, mental, and physical fitness for her God-given task] And makes her arms strong.

¹⁸ She sees that her gain is good; Her lamp does not go out, but it burns continually through

the night [she is prepared for whatever lies ahead].

¹⁹ She stretches out her hands to the distaff, And her hands hold the spindle [as she spins wool into thread for clothing].

²⁰ She opens and extends her hand to the poor, And she reaches out her filled hands to the needy.

²¹ She does not fear the snow for her household, For all in her household are clothed in [expensive] scarlet

[wool].

²² She makes for herself coverlets, cushions, and rugs of tapestry. Her clothing is linen, pure and fine, and purple [wool].

²³ Her husband is known in the [city's] gates, When he sits among the elders of the land.

²⁴ She makes [fine] linen garments and sells them; And supplies sashes to the merchants.

²⁵ Strength and dignity are her clothing and her position is strong and secure; And she smiles at the future [knowing that she and her family are prepared]

WHY?

²⁶ She opens her mouth in [skillful and godly] wisdom, And the teaching of kindness is on her tongue [giving counsel and instruction].

²⁷ She looks well to how things go in her household and does not eat the bread of idleness.

²⁸ Her children rise up and call her blessed (happy, prosperous, to be admired); Her husband also, and he praises her, saying,

²⁹ "Many daughters have done nobly, and well [with the strength of character that is steadfast in goodness], But you excel them all."

³⁰ Charm and grace are deceptive, and [superficial] beauty is vain, but a woman who fears the Lord [reverently worshiping, obeying, serving, and trusting Him with awe-filled respect], she shall be praised.

³¹ Give her of the product of her hands, and let her own works praise her in the gates [of the city].

The question has always been who can find a proverbs 31 woman. After this makeover, I stand to ask who has her? And we together will say our Heavenly Father...

CHAPTER 4

Do Marriages Fail or Do People Fail Marriages?

This is such a complex question/statement. Who gets into anything to fail? If failure occurs, then who's to blame? Well, let's pull it apart and see what causes failure in marriages.

When you chose your mate, I'm sure it's with forever in mind, which includes ups and downs ins and outs. Well, that would depend on the other person as well. Let's lay out a few reasons things go wrong or right. Hey, for the sake of argument, let's do right first. You say 'I will' to you don't know what. Let's be upfront about it. We really don't know what we've just committed ourselves to. All we do know is we want to give our all, and for the most part, that's true but not so realistic. Why? Because everyone has a free-will and thoughts that you can't know unless it's shared with you.

I remember my husband telling me years later on in our marriage that the day of our wedding, he said to himself that he would give it five years and if it didn't work, then he was out. I was like, "What! You thought that?"

So, I said that to say we all have inward thoughts at the beginning that we, for the most part, don't share with our new mate. It's like a secret escape door that only you know about. If things turn out okay, then you don't have to use it. If things go sour fast, then things will go bump in the night as you make your grand escape. Life begins to happen, and your little differences begin to show up, like the way you keep up the house or how each other spends money. You begin thinking of your own future and start setting self-goals without talking it over. You stop working on your goals and laziness kicks in. I mean, should you have to share this type of information with your spouse? I mean, your goals and visions right. What about wanting to start a family or not at all, change of mind, weight gain or not enough weight in the hips, butt, breast, or thigh areas, or family issues.

You don't pray together anymore or now you want to pray together. You slow down on reading your Bible. You try to settle into this new relationship ,so you haven't been to church like you were once going. Oh, the list could really go on but here we see how the real you shows up. Sometimes you start out okay with the little things and maybe it's not a problem for you, but it is a problem for Father God. If it's a problem for Him, well, then it's going to be a problem for both of you.

Often times, people aren't in the wrong relationship. They are just not aligned with the Power Source that will bring forth the power that's needed to see where they are headed, so it causes them to bump into each other. Things start to hurt after so many bumps and within that time of darkness, you really see what's down in there. It's like someone who has poor eyesight who drives in the day time. You notice that their driving is more than a little bit off, but you don't want to make them feel like you don't trust them, so you go along for the ride, all the while cringing on the inside and waiting for the ride to be over. Instead of telling them that they suck at driving, you play it off. When they ask, "Why every time it's time to leave you run to the driver seat?" and you say, "Well, I just want to drive," and you've been saying this all along.

Then one day, you have an argument as it relates to trust, and you reference that person's driving. You tell them how you really feel about their driving. Now they are really on the fence about the argument because you allowed them to think that you trusted them when you really didn't. See, we often do this with people, especially our spouses, and allow them to believe one thing when you clearly feel another way. When does the truth come out about how you really feel? In a heated argument, when feelings are all over the place. The thing about it is that the person denies the fact about what you said about their driving. When the problem just might be poor eyesight or forethought which everyone it has caused both now not to trust each other.

The enemy of your marriage only needs a small crack to get in and try to take over. I'm not necessarily saying that you should see if the person can drive before you say I do or you do, but it wouldn't hurt. What I am saying is to be upfront on how you feel and don't allow someone to think one way when you are clearly feeling another way. Often times if we say something upfront or when we first notice, we can avoid the crazies. When or spouse doesn't meet our expectations, it drops concern in our mind. If we don't catch it, then the thought travels to our heart for a later time, and that, for the most part, is not a good thing.

The Word of God says this in Song of Solomon 2:15 (AMP), "My heart was touched and I fervently sang to him my desire] Take for us the foxes, the little foxes that spoil the vineyards [of our love], for our vineyards are in blossom."

Here you see that if you don't deal with your issues upfront, they become like foxes. The foxes will spoil that which you need and love. These little foxes take on all sorts of forms. It can be anywhere from money, trust, sex, religion, children, careers, family, friends, education, ideas, vision, sickness and any kind of addiction. If you don't deal with it, then it will turn into a fox and take what's of great value. If you don't catch them, they will destroy the vine, and it can take some time to fix the problem and begin to see fruit again.

Father God knows that these types of issues are waiting behind your veil and this nice little bow tie, and He's not afraid to deal with them head-on. Yes, you might not like what you see or feel in the other person. You might even say, "I didn't sign up for this," but if this is the person

Father God has in mind for you, then you would do yourself a huge favor by sitting down because trust me. Your turn is coming up next for it is within these issues the Father gets His raw material to build with the union He had in mind from the beginning. You can trust Him.

You might say, "Well, how come I didn't see this at first?" or "Why didn't God fix this before we got married?" Well, if it's any consolation, Adam was perfect until he woke up. Smile!! Do you get the point? Father God sometimes waits for the right one to get close to you so that He can work out His will in you. We all are perfect until we encounter another human. Marriage is Father God's union, so we must allow Him to run His show and dress us for His stage.

Look at it this way: you find out the script to your role and learn your part and allow the director to correct any mistakes so that you can be at peace with your castmate. Have you ever gone to a rehearsal of any kind and seen it all over the place and people were all in their feelings? No one knew their parts. No one was dressed properly. No one showed up for dress rehearsal, and then who do they blame? The director. Until the director shows up and begins to ask them questions and checking their to-do list, you will quickly see who's at fault. You see this at its best here in Genesis 3:12-13, "And the man said, the woman whom You gave to be with me—she gave me [fruit] from the tree, and I ate. And the Lord God said to the woman, what is this you have done? And the woman said, the serpent beguiled (cheated, outwitted, and deceived) me, and I ate."

No matter who's to blame, only the one who wrote the script can fix it. So why won't we save ourselves the trouble and do what He says from the beginning?? You are a WIP - a work in progress - so be of good cheer. Father God is well aware of who and what you married... I meant who you are. Just a little humor!! If you are willing to walk in the grace of God in Jesus Christ by the Holy Spirit, then you are well on your way. But if you are going to do it the world's way, then you get what you get, and you have no right to complain to the Father because you keep choosing to do it without Him. Only His way is fail-proof and that's according to His standards and His will. You will quickly learn that sometimes the will of the Father can be painful. Job 13:15 says, "Even though He kills me; I will hope in Him. Nevertheless, I will argue my ways to His face."

See when you trust in the ways of the Father, then this will easily become your confession. It doesn't mean you understand or agree with his methods. It just means no matter what form of method used, you won't back out on Him, and you will remain faithful to your spouse and Your Father. Keep in mind that the Father loves you both!

CHAPTER 5

Vision Versus Vision

Vision- Unusual competence in discernment or perception; intelligent foresight.

Vision in anything is good, but how do we know that we are carrying out the right vision for our lives and marriages? Well, easy. We don't until we go through something and it doesn't line up with the vision of your heart or Father God's.

GOD HAS A VISION FOR MARRIAGE

How do I receive a vision for my marriage? Good question. Happy you asked because, so few do. Simple! JUST ASK. Now be ready to do the work. Yes, marriage is work. Tearing down and building up one another is dangerous and powerful at the same time. Also, necessary.

See both of you have your understanding of marriage. It is based on a few things:
1. How you were taught.
2. What you think of the opposite sex.
3. Your understanding of marriage.
4. Your reason for wanting to be married.

These are just a few items on the list.

Hear me and hear me well! How someone thinks is very crucial because it is those thoughts that will lead to one's actions, be it bad or good. We have said so many times that it doesn't matter what you think, or they think and leave it there, but I declare to you it does! How it does! It is dangerous to deny the power of one's own thoughts. It is within the heart of the man that you say you love and want to be with forever and he will lead and cover you with those thoughts. People last or fail on thoughts. Kingdoms were brought to nothing because someone had a thought to destroy it.

HOW TO KNOW HIS THOUGHTS!

Yes, girl, now you are talking! I would love to know his every thought and more. Yeah, I know right! NOT! It is not our right or place to know his every thought or his to know yours. Sorry ladies. That PLACE BELONGS TO THE LORD ALONE.

God himself will reveal his motives to you and what to do in the moment. The Lord will guide you through your husband's desires, for it was the Lord who said your desire will be unto your husband. Genesis 3:16 states so. Knowing the mind of God is just as important. There are some hard things in His word, but nevertheless it must be obeyed.

Please understand this point here. I'm not saying these things to push you away from marriage, but I want you to have a clear understanding of what is to be expected of you both at all times, on good days and not so good days.

Why marry and hope for success when you can guarantee success. DISCLAIMER! That does not mean you will not have hard times and growing pain. You are bringing two people into a God covenant that can only be governed by Him. If we try and do it without Him, well, let's say it this way. Why be married for 5, 10, 15,20, 30, or 60 years and can't stand each other and hold on to what? By now, you would probably be saying who and what am I married to. And yes, we are still talking about vision and thoughts.

Ladies, we are good at counting and shopping, right? Yes! So, let's use that to our advantage and not our disadvantage. Well, Yushonda, whatever do you mean? Happy you asked once again.

You could have firsthand knowledge of what's going on in your marriage ⏃ and in your relationship with the Holy Spirit. He will begin to download strategy on how you should pray. He will also begin to show you things to come and plans that he has for you and your husband. He will also show you things to get involved in and stay away from and how to prayer proof your house. He will show you the family vision and the history as well as the future. He will awaken your senses to the invisible world.

The Holy Spirit is all-knowing. When you come into the understanding that the Holy Spirit is for you and not against you, you will be amazed at how He speaks to you. You can trust Him. He cares and wants you to have a successful marriage, but you must do things His way. He will show you things about yourself, as well. So often we ask for someone else to change, but God is a well-rounded God. If you are going to function properly in your marriage, then He's going to perform a little heart surgery on you first.

I WAS WELL UNTIL I MET YOU!!

See, we think that all was well until we said I do. How far from the truth, that is? When you are self- centered, you tend to think everyone has a problem but you. I mean, who's going to tell you that you stink if there's no one to smell it. Who will challenge you to share if there's no one there to ask? When would you say I'm sorry if no one was there to say you hurt their feelings?

See, the Holy Spirit will use our closest family members to bring about a change. Hear me when I say it doesn't get 'realer' than a spouse and children!! Forget the dog!! Husbands have a way of bringing out the best of the worst in us wives. Oh, yes, they are gifted in this area. Well learned!! Ok, you get my point.

See, when it's just you, everything is okay. There's nothing wrong with what you say or do because no one sees or hears you but you. You have been that way for so long until you think the problem areas are someone else's. But oh, how Holy Spirit will shine the light on that and when He does, He will also replace it with what He wants for your life. He will keep in mind the other person as well. Remember, we are in time. Father God isn't, so He is working outside of our time, which means it will take some time, so be patient with each other.

I can't express that enough. We want things right now and that won't carry in this union. We will have to pray our husbands through, ladies. How can you properly pray for him if you are complaining or if you are always in your feelings? All you do is talk about what is wrong, what he did this time, how much it hurts, it's unfair, and the beat goes on. But when will you stop and realize that you are getting more of what it is you don't want based upon what continues to come out of your mouth, and then you add too many feelings with it?

You share your issues with the wedding party in the form of friends and I sure hope for your sake, there's a least one friend willing to tell you to "SHUT UP GIRL AND PRAY!" And if you don't have those kinds of friends, then I will be your friend, okay? SHUT UP! Your words have power. Use that time in prayer.

Did you know that when you talk about your husband to others, it breaks his trust for you? You are talking about him while he is in a tough place.

If you want him to trust you with his issues, then you might want to learn this word fast and rush to put it into practice: CONFIDENTIALITY. If you are going to be used to heal your marriage, then you are going to have to show yourself trustworthy.

Yes, there will come a time when you will need someone to talk to but let that be a person of wisdom and someone who doesn't mind saying the two-word phrase: SHUT UP!!

Holy Spirit is highly equipped to handle all things. ALL, if you allow Him to. Greater is waiting on the other side, and remember, you never know when it will be your turn. So, do unto him as you would have him do unto you. It's just that simple!!

CHAPTER 6

Advantage Versus Disadvantage

Now, ladies, you must admit, we like to know before we know, right?! I mean, that's like the new fade being in the know zone.

We want to know what's about to happen beforehand so that we can be prepared for it. That's just how we are wired, and that isn't a bad thing in its proper usage. Allow me to explain.

See, we as women are naturally intuitive when it comes down to knowing, especially when it comes to those closest to us or around us. With that, we see things going on behind the scenes.

Good Father God has given us that for a reason. It goes along with our caring nature and if we look at it Father God's way, it's Him allowing us in on the board meeting of the affairs of our family, friends, and sometimes total strangers. And when we use this to our advantage in prayer and not gossip, then we can bring about mighty changes.

I remember when the Lord began to alert me on some family issues. I was all over the place. I thought because He was showing me that, if I prayed and did what

He said, then the worst wouldn't happen. Well, that was far from my truth. This brings to mind the passage in Isaiah 55:8-9

[8] For My thoughts are not your thoughts, neither are your ways My ways, says the Lord. [9] For as the heavens are higher than the earth, so are My ways higher than your ways and My thoughts than your thoughts...

I remember being so upset. Not so much at what happened but because He showed me what was going to happen and what was on the brink of happening. But Father had something far greater in mind than what I had been shown in the spirit.

The sooner we understand that, we will do well and become more effective in prayer and in the role Father God has called us to and the Holy Spirit can do some mighty things with us as women, wives, mothers, and friends. Let's not allow our need to know put us in a bad way with the Father.

See, with the Holy Spirit, we never have to be left out of the loop unless it's His will not to share, but for the most part, we will have heads up on our family business as it relates to their walk in life. I can't begin to tell you how worry-free I live because I have taught and put a demand on myself to trust in the Holy Spirit for all wisdom and knowledge in raising my family. He has been faithful to do just that and then some.

See, you have been positioned to win, but self-practice, flesh, and the enemy don't want you to win at this. The enemy wants you to think that you are always at a disadvantage when it comes down to your relationships and it will come in the form of a Husband. It may seem as if he's just never going to change, you will never be good enough to do that or it's too hard, the kids just hate you and you don't want to lose them by pushing them into or out of harm's way or maybe hoping they will get it on their own or whichever way it comes. I'm here to tell you, ladies, your greatest power is to pray your husband through. You must become his sergeant and birth him out and pushing can really hurt. The pain is great, but the joy of what's to come is greater. The Holy Spirit will show you how to carry and tarry with your husband in the spirit.

He might not even know at first that you are even praying for him and trust me, he might not think much of it at first, but don't allow that to concern you. Your job is to pray, and don't you stop. His life will depend on it. You are not called to pray for your family as if it's some magic wand. You don't like this or that, so you are just going to pray, and Father God is just going to change everything about them that you don't like or that what you don't care for.

No, ma'am, that's not how it works at all. Now somethings the Lord will have you praying about just might be on your to-do list for your family, but the Lord is working on something greater than your 'honey do' list. In the form of I'm praying for all I don't like.

Within this union, the Lord is also working on you and His relationship as well, so be mindful and keep under yourself and remember 1 John 4:4: Greater is he that's within you than he who is in the world.

CHAPTER 7

Whose Identity Are You Marrying Into?

Your marriage doesn't have to look like no one else's but yours, and you won't know what that looks like until you are headed down the road of faith. Trust me, it's never what it seems at first sight. Now, this isn't always a bad thing. This madness has its perks. Put it this way: if things are kind of off at first, then you know what to work on. If they are well put together, then you know what's going to be tested.

Being tested in your marriage will come at you both in all sorts of ways. You will feel at times that you have married the wrong person and at others, you will feel like he or she is clearly working for the devil, but that's far from the truth. What you will be dealing with is self-images that you and your spouse have allowed into your minds and God will challenge that for the making of you both.

See, we so often want the other person fixed so that we can feel better, but in most cases, it's us. We have to be conformed into the image of Christ. My friend, the Lord uses those closest to us to bring that work about. It is through this kind of testing that you really see you and whose you really are. It's very easy to bring this process in with this thought, "I was doing fine until you..." But it's all a part of the plan of God, for He has an image that He is working on as well.

He loves you and He has vested somethings in you that you know nothing of. You say, "Well, why test me through my marriage? Won't He just tell me, and I will comply?" and I say, "Yeah right," cause if it was that easy, then it would already be done.

God is all-knowing and He knows well and well. As soon as the heat is turned up on you and your spouse, the most loving, patient and kind will run! Why? Because it's hot! And guess what? He will turn it up hotter and hotter just to get the glory. Remember it's His covenant that you have joined yourselves to, not the other way around. Look at it this way: if you are renting out property and you want to make some changes, you will ask for permission of the ones you are renting to before you can make necessary changes to your unit, or will you notify them of the changes that are to come? 'Lord' means just that: OWNER! This means there is some work to do and it will get nasty. Things will be all over the place just to bring about the remodel the Lord is looking for. The finished work will be worth it if you allow Him to redefine you in His fire!

Your Marriage is more than just two people who desire to spend their life together, for generations are birth out of unions like this one. That's why it is so important that we allow the Holy Spirit to have His way. Bloodlines carry so much potential but so much mess is running over and through it. If we are not careful, we will keep reproducing more mess and that's not the will of God for your bloodline.

You will produce offspring for the Lord as well, and there is a certain way they must be conceived, carried, birth out and raised. That's also true for you, spiritual parents. Not all couples will bring forth natural children and that will be a matter of your and your husband's hearts. The Lord will minister to you both and especially if you really want children.

Remember, His ways are far greater than ours were, but He will see you through it all. Don't be dismayed and don't allow the enemy of your marriage to cause you to speak against Father God and His will for your marriage. Your reward is greater in heaven than ten sons. The Holy Spirit has a way of settling the matters of the heart, even when we don't understand.

A transparent moment here. I remember when my husband and I were wanting more children, and so we did what was natural to us. I had gotten pregnant and we were like, "Yes! First try bam!" My husband's birthday was coming up and we wanted to go out that night for dinner and a movie. So, while we were out at dinner, my stomach began to hurt. I told him that I was ready to go, but we needed to stop by Walmart first. I told my husband that I was going to go to the restroom and so I went. Now, ladies, you know how we hate to sit on public restroom seats, right? Okay, well, I lined the toilet, but I didn't sit on it. I saw blood when I started peeing. The next thing I felt was a big push come down and I heard a loud drop into the toilet. As soon as I felt that, I knew right away that it was my baby. The most dawning part for me was that it was the kind of toilet that automatically flushed, and it happened so fast. I almost fainted!!!!!

All I wanted was my husband. I couldn't believe what had just happened to me — talking about feeling hopeless. I was beyond hopeless and when I ran out that restroom, my husband said, "Baby, you look like someone just died," and I just broke down crying uncontrollably. When I finally could talk, I told him what had just happened. He was at a loss for three days. I didn't eat, sleep, or talk. I could do nothing but cry and ask God why.

Why even allow me to get pregnant just to let that happen and in that way? And then on my husband's birthday? Days later, the Lord would speak. His words didn't make sense to me, but His voice brought me such comfort. I know that sounds crazy, but it did. This is what He said to me in the time of my pain and confusion. "That was the only way that you could handle it, but you will keep the next one." I was like what?? But He made good on what He said and since then I have had two boys. You might not understand His ways but when I tell you that you can trust Him, you truly can. No greater hands to be in, for He was there through it all.

CHAPTER 8

Who's Wearing The Secret Parachute In This Marriage?

Isn't this till death do us part? Well, I'm not ready to die just yet. Yeah, that's going to leave a mark. The feeling of betrayal you feel when you think that your marriage is one way and it's really another. It seems as if we forgot to ask a few more questions on our dates or maybe we didn't go on enough. Maybe none. When you said, "I do," it was for the long haul, right?

Well, what do you do when you are with the one God has for you, but they are living like and acting as if you are Leah instead of Rachel? Well, that's a clear indication that this one is going to be some work. Yes, work! Do not, I repeat, do not retract your vows to the Lord. But what if he wants to leave because he doesn't want to do it Father God's way? Then I say to you, let him go. I didn't say get rid of him but don't fight him on his free will. Tell him, "I will not hold you against your free will, but you do not have my agreement to break covenant vows," and allow Father God to work His will out in that and be mindful of your words, for they can make or break you.

I keep hearing that Laban spirit and how he tricked Jacob in Genesis 25: 19-34. Keep in mind that Jacob was a trickster as well, and he got that from his mother. Remember that Jacob and Esau were twins and how their mother thought of a plan to trick their father concerning the birthright of the twins. Jacob agreed and helped trick him out of his birthright. Well, the same thing happened to Jacob. He had rightfully earned Rachel, but he got Leah instead. Sometimes our spouses are not aware of the spiritual attacks that are coming against them. Sometimes neither one will understand what's going on, and the Holy Spirit will send someone your way to teach you or lead you to a book such as this one just to let you know that He is working in and on your behalf.

Books nor people take the place of the Holy Spirit in our affairs. He just uses them until you can hear on your own and trust His voice and His ways. You don't have to run when the enemy comes in. That's the time to call upon the Lord and He will put the enemy to flight. You just be sure that your obedience is in place. Let's fight the Good Fight and not against!

CHAPTER 9

Knowing Your Man

What does the word Man mean to you? What is a Man? A man exemplifies masculine qualities. So, there are sure qualities that a man carries that we as women should beware of. Usually, you would begin to see this modeled in your life as a little girl: your father, grandfather, uncles, brothers, cousins, etc., all of which are relational. Within these different forms of relationships, you should also see how a woman should or shouldn't respond or carry herself around men.

So often, we see misleading examples of what this should look like. We are products of our own environment. If mama didn't like you, then the children didn't either. How the women in our lives behaved themselves intentionally or unintentionally around men became a point of reference for us. It scoped our behavior with our counterparts or partners called men.

I remember seeing a very close female family member with the love of her life in action. The look of love was all in her face. I looked with excitement with and for her. I remember thinking, "Wow! This must be love." But later, I learned that he was everybody's man. I was at a loss for what I had witnessed and interpreted as love.

I thought because she was so happy with him that it must be right for them and maybe he wasn't happy at home. I would later find out that this man had a thing for all types of women and home wasn't the issue. Lust was.

But you see how that was acted out in front of me as a young girl? If I wasn't taught better and learned that was wrong and not the way to a godly relationship, I would be a victim to the same lifestyle or worse. Like the woman who is home waiting for her boyfriend or husband to come off the neighborhood watch. Men in their need to explore their sexuality can make a bad name for themselves, but for some reason, they get a pass by saying, "Well, that's just a man for you." It's so far from the truth. Men who lay around are just as broken as the women they are sleeping with. Both are the walking dead and all along the enemy of their souls are creating situations in them that will have to be dealt with in marriage and their relationship with Father God.

Men are meant to provide, protect, groom, nurture, build, and destroy. That's just man principle 101 alone. If they are broken and spread thin within their soul, that will make it harder to see marriage through Father God's eyes, and his flesh will always want more.

What do I mean by more? When a man, according to the Word of Father God lays with a woman, he gives his strength away. Proverbs 31:3 says, "Give not your strength to (loose) women, nor your ways to those who and that ruin and destroy kings."

Men, for the most part, are taught that it's okay to see what's out there and they go out on the hunt. They become bound, entangled in generational curses, and are not aware of how to get loose. They bring these different soul ties into their marriage unaware. Men, for the most part, can lay with a woman and when they have released themselves, they are done. But that is so far from the truth. Men are very valuable to us. We should care about the seed and vision God has put in them.

Now, if you notice here, I listed some of a man's God-inherited qualities that should be well in operation long before he starts trying to work on you. I mean, if he's not using these principles on himself, he won't use them on you right away. This is how women get caught because we see the potential in a man and we figure if we just love him, and help him, then he will do right by us. Here is a little nugget on that note: God himself will be the only one able to use him in his full capacity. Why? Because everything about him came from the Father himself and unless he goes back to the source of his blueprint, you and he both are at risk of spiritual and a natural death.

Man needs God for his very footing. Be mindful of men who are leery or runners from the Father because what that is saying is, "I don't need or want you. I have no need for you." If he has no need for God, then he has no need for you. What I mean by that is this: God created man to work the vision that was in his heart as it is in heaven, so shall it be here on earth. Man needs some major help, so then here we come, Woman, to help the man who had the plan, the blueprint, and the layout: not the 'get me out, I can't figure it out, and I won't out' syndrome.

Ladies, you are going to have to be needed in order to be necessary for a man! No vision! No wife! It's because of a lack of vision on both parties that you find yourself in a downward spiral with no way out seemingly. For a man not to know His vision is harmful to him because he is open to the vision of the enemy to his soul.

Man shall not live by bread alone but by every word that proceeds out of the mouth of God. And when he seeks for a wife and finds her, then he obtains favor from her Father and only Father God can give a prudent wife. He or she can lack anything because both are the very purpose of God in action. When the gates of hell try to come against what God has joined together, the Father will defend them. That's the real meaning because man has his vision from Father God first, then he goes back to Father God for a suitable helpmate, and the Lord gives him a wife according to the blueprint in his heart. Why wouldn't we want that kind of success? Wow! That just took me down.

We think that marriage is all about us and our human ideas and feelings of 'I love you,' babies, and the big wedding day. Let's crack this nut and get to the real meaning and purpose of this thing called marriage. It's time to be wise about marriage and stop being hypersensitive about how he or she looks, how sex is going to be, where are we going to live, how many babies we can have, who will see us, and let's not forget about self-gain.

Now it's time to ask Father God how He feels about you marrying now because we fail to realize that we belong to Him. When we bring outside people into our relationship with Him without His permission, then that's trespassing. We are in direct violation and now we must be dealt with. You are for God or against Him, so we must check in with Him. For us not to is detrimental to us as well as others.

We've heard for so long that's it's your life, it's better to marry than to burn and the list goes on and on. Until now, marriage is looked at as having legal sex. So, you fill your heart up with lust for someone that Father God never gave you permission to marry in the first place. When He tells you no, you throw a fit and go find someone who is spiritually dead that thinks he or she knows the voice of Father and by doing so they consent to your rebellion. They tell you that marriage is honorable, and the bed is undefiled. All along, you know in your heart that it is a NO!

But your flesh and outside voices convince you that God is in it. As if Father God can't see what you see and clearly doesn't understand how much you want this man to be your husband. You will pay a heavy price for your disobedience to the very will of Father God. You could cause your children to be in ruins when you deny the will of Father God to be at work in your life. So, Father God must work out His will the other way and it won't be so well for you.

What does a man with a God-given vision look like? A man that knows the will of God for his life will be at work on it. When you meet him, the Holy Spirit will reveal it to you. You will conceive his vision within your womb, and you will start to give birth to what it is that he carries. Now let me share this with you. Sometimes your husband won't naturally look like what it is that he would become, but the Lord will give you a heart for his purpose. He will teach you how to birth him out and push him through in prayer. Sometimes all they really need is a good push.

The Holy Spirit will confirm if he's the one. Father God won't play games with you. Let's keep in mind, just because something doesn't last doesn't mean you got it wrong. That is why you must understand the type of woman you are. All women are not the same. Why would the Lord put a baker with a mechanic? Or a hairdresser with a fisherman? They are going into two different directions. You will be incompatible with each other. If there is a difference between the two, it won't be a big difference. It will complement each other, but that doesn't mean that God has not given you vision. Sometimes you will have the leading role within the vision.

Now that does not say that you are greater than your husband. It's just that the Lord will use you as the package sometimes, but your husband will also be within the wrapping. We must be mindful in this type of situation because the enemy of your marriage will try and use this type of situation against you to bring in jealousy. If you are not watchful and in prayer, it will work.

You are a team! No one is left out of the wrapping. The wrapping is not more important than what is in packaging. Both are necessary for delivery. Teach each other, work with the Holy Spirit, build your family and the kingdom of God. People need to see couples that can be selfless and allow the Holy Spirit to take control. You both are great together. Just remain in your lane and do the work of the one that has called you two together in the first place.

CHAPTER 10

Whose Idea Was This?

Marriage is for mankind, but it did not originate from us. God Himself is the author of the union that we humans so ignorantly enter into with disregard to the owner. 'How to be' can be very strong in its usage because it suggests that there is a 'how not to be.' Let's get into how we, as women sometimes allow ourselves to be prepared for marriage.

There are several ways to prepare one's self for a husband. Let's look at them closely and see if you see yourself in any of the examples. It's okay to self-examine. You might find out somethings about yourself that's been tucked away for so long that it's asking to be dealt with. Women, we look at the man we would like to marry. We look at the kind of dress and ring. We even go as far as to plan out a special honeymoon to seal the deal. But how many times did we include the Father on our plans?

Did you know that it is the father of the bride to be who pays for everything? Do you know why? It was traditions and the fact that in biblical times, a daughter was like property to a family. Great value was put on the son and not so much the daughter. But that's man's way of thinking, not Father God. He loves us, His daughters, oh how He loves us! We are a joy and a gift to have, even to the point that He doesn't leave us when He allows us to marry, for it is within His plans for our life. Do you think that the Father will just turn you over to someone and walk away? Too funny! NEVER! It is He that makes us into helpful helpmates. Therefore, we should never move into any relationship without talking it over with our beloved Father God because it does matter. He cares more than we could ever know.

When the Father gives you to be a bride, He expects to gain a Godly offspring from your union. That's why it is deadly to seek out your own husband. He that finds a wife (Proverbs 18:22), meaning he, the man, will seek out your Heavenly Father for your hand in marriage.

You just continue to stay in the presence of the Father and get your training and counseling. The Lord expects great things from us as women. It is He that has designed us the way that we are and not us ourselves. Only He knows the reason and usage of us: from the color of our skin, to the length of our hair, to the frame of our hips, to the natural smell of our skin, to our breasts, to the tone of our voice, and the lips that he will kiss.

It is our Heavenly Father that made us women, not man. The Lord doesn't want us to get so caught up on the outer shell until we fail to see our inner selves. For in this, ladies, has Father God suffered great loss. We as His daughters refuse to keep ourselves and remain chaste. We are flaunting around and not carrying ourselves as virgins and daughters of the highest king and God. Then we allow our flesh to dictate to our souls. Then we give ourselves to men who not only didn't have permission to have us but can care less about our Father. We give them our virtue and produce bastards for offsprings, but that's another lesson within itself. No one wants to think of a sweet little baby as a bastard. I'm looking at it not from an earthly point, but a spiritual point of view.

Bloodlines are highly important to Father God. You can see it up and down in the Bible verses. It should be important to you. Father God has a plan that He is working out in us, so don't think that you know more than He does or that it doesn't matter. Take out the time and ask Father what He thinks. What does He want? Trust me. He will lead you in the pathway that's best for you according to His perfect will for your life. Why call Him Lord, if you were going to do it your own way? God, the Father, is rich in His love, grace, and mercy. He can't fail at this so you might as well let Him have His way in you. Now let the real work begin.

CHAPTER 11

The World's Way Or Your Way?

Women, we are going to have to make a choice every day on how we are going to live out our days as wives because life will happen. You are going to respond and feel some kind of way. Do you not know subconsciously you are being programmed to handle life's issues already? Even before it happens to you! We must ask the Holy Spirit to help us govern our thoughts and feelings, especially as it relates to our husbands and children, as well as those that are connected to us. Women, we all want to be looked at as a woman who makes things happen and to be known for supporting our husbands. Sometimes in doing so, we can lose ourselves because we are so used to being everything to everybody plus all the other things that we are involved in. We need the Holy Spirit because after you have given, no one takes notice to see that you need to be poured back into.

It's going to go south real fast if you don't govern your emotions and activities. I mean, we don't have to play the role of 'I have it all together' as if nothing bothers us. I remember calling a family meeting and telling everyone that they did not have my permission to mistreat me! I wanted my family to know that while I was in my right mind and not when something crazy happens as it sometimes will. Then I went down a list of things that I considered as mistreatment. When they crossed the line, I made sure they knew it, how it made me feel, and the consequences for mistreating me. We have to be well-rounded women, wives and mothers to function in the capacity as Father God would have us to. It's not all about the family alone and you just fall by the wayside. The devil is a liar. We have dreams and goals as well. That's why you must know your worth, ladies, for this life and its roles are temporal.

The Holy Spirit will show and tell you how to manage your household and its affairs. If you are out of sync with Him, then you will be out of sync with your husband and children. Your husband could be dealing with some financial issues that he might not know how to tell you about. If you start noticing subtle changes in his behavior, then you start feeling like he's holding back something from you. It might be so, but your husband's plans are to fix the issue without telling you. For in his mind, he's a man first and he can handle it. But in the midst of dealing with what it is, he starts to tell you about your spending habits then stops making money available to you like you were used to.

See all these things are triggers and tools for the enemy to come in, who causes confusion, destroys your trust, and steal your peace and joy.

But if you are communing with the Holy Spirit, He will let you know what's really going on in your home and the plans of the enemy to attack you or your husband. If the Holy Spirit doesn't give you a heads up on the issue right away, it is because He's trying to show you something about yourself. These issues will become mirrors in your relationship with your husband, children and Father God. Sometimes we are not the way we think we are.

Sometimes we think that we are doing it God's way when really, it's our way because we fail to ask Him how to handle daily situations. Then we are all over the place in our thoughts, feelings, and sometimes, even our bodies began to hurt. Father God will allow you and your husband to go through a season of trials and tests just to reveal to you what's in your hearts. He will observe how you treat one another and Himself as well. The Father will allow some tough stuff to hit your house. You will think it's the devil but it's really the Lord reproving and approving you. Yeah, I've heard that question? What if he doesn't believe like I do or at all? What if his faith is shaky to the point you wonder if he even wants a relationship with the Lord anymore? Ladies, I will be the first to say, if the Lord said yes and is still saying yes, then it's YES! If God has not changed His mind about your husband, then you shouldn't either. Now you must make up in your mind how you are going to feel. Get in the face of God and do business.

There will be some tests that will come and shake you to your core and you will want to throw in the towel, just drop it all, leave it all, and start over. But when you understand that you have more than one man that you married and said yes to, then you won't be so quick to abandon ship. There is one more feeling involved in this relationship who stands to lose or gain. Remember Father God is working out His perfect will in and through you and your husband and if you give up, how will it ever come to pass.

What if Mary told the Angel Gabriel that she was too young to be a mother or that she was about to get married and voiced her thoughts on how she would look to everyone else? If she agreed to this plan in secret, would shame and hurt be caused publicly? See the Lord will allow some of your stuff to hit Front Street and tell you His grace is sufficient for in all things.

For so many reasons, the Lord will allow drama to hit our houses for His Glory. Let's join in on the plan, not against it, because it starts to hurt or pull you out of shape. You are pregnant with your destiny. Keep pushing. It hurts now but it won't after a while. Greater is coming, in Jesus' name.

When you are in tune with the Holy Spirit and began spending time with Him, you will start to have strong feelings for Him. You will even begin to have a strong bond and respect for Him like no other to the point you don't want to disappoint Him or leave Him out. As a matter of fact, He will be the first person you run to. He will be there and began to download a strategy in your spirit about your issues. As I have stated before, you might not understand His ways at times, but you can trust them.

He will not change His way of doing things to fit our understanding. We are speaking about Father God who brought all things into existence.

He spoke the heavens and set the boundaries in place for the oceans and seas that they still obey. Think on that the next time you see a big body of water and it stays in place.

Women we look at the man we would like to marry. We look at the dress and ring, so why would we deny the Father to look into the decision with us. He knows the way that we should take. Trust Him and He will lead the way. Now let's get married for real! Congratulations! To the Father of the bride.

The end.

About The Author

Just when Yushonda thought all the troubles of her childhood were out the way, through the tumultuous vicissitudes of her childhood, she heard the voice of God reveal to her the husband that He promised her at the tender yet stress-filled age of 15. A "door prize" of sorts that she joyfully accepted for all the hell she had been through as a young adolescent child.

As time passed and life unfolded, she would come to know the Father by His voice versus the move of His hand. It was that same voice that confirmed her husband; the same voice that guided her through the roughest time in her adult life. Simultaneously, His hand was clearing the path for victory at every seemingly impossible situation.

A mother of seven and a wife of 17 years to a wonderful man, provider, and father, a non-profit organization leader, and homeschooler from Atlanta, GA, had to find a way to mitigate the drama in her present life that stemmed from her stormy childhood. She needed the redeeming feature that would help her virtuously build her family instead of tearing it apart continuing into a dark and cold destiny. She found it. Moreover, she went through a great amount of detail explaining how it changed her life outlining key turning points and valuable principles in this book.

The redeeming feature of her life has occurred by involving another husband. The journey begins here...

Index

A

argument, 34, 36–37

B

behavior, 23, 65, 80
belief system, 25
birthright, 63
bloodline, 58, 77
breasts, 35, 76
bride, 75–76, 84

C

capacity, 68, 80
confusion, 60, 80
counsel, 8, 32
couples, 58, 72
covenant, 2, 57
covenant vows, 16
creator, 25, 28

D

darkness, 20–21, 36
death, 61
destiny, 20, 83
devil, 56, 80–81
disappointments, 27
disobedience, 71
distractions, 27
drama, 83, 86
dysfunction, 23

E

emotions, 13, 79
enemy, 14, 37, 53, 58, 63, 66, 68, 72, 80–81

evil, 6, 30

F

failure, 33–34
faith, 55, 81
fight, 62–63
financial issues, 80
flesh, 7, 25, 53, 66, 70, 77
friendships, 28
fruit, 38, 40

G

generational curses, 67
glory, 23, 57, 83
grace, 32, 40, 77, 83

H

hate, 53, 59
heart, 7, 12, 14, 22, 26, 29, 37–38, 42–43, 59, 68–71, 81
heartbreaks, 8
heavens, 7, 52, 58, 68, 84
hell, 69, 85

helpmates, 69, 75
Holy Spirit, 17–18, 28, 40, 45–47, 49, 52–53, 58, 63, 71–73, 79–81, 83
home, 12, 16, 65–66, 81
honeymoon, 16
hopeless, 60
household, 30–32, 80
hypersensitive, 69

I

Ignorance, 17
imaginations, 6
impatient, 27–28
inheritance, 19
institution, 28
instruction, 32

J

jealousy, 6, 72
joy, 18–20, 23, 25, 53, 75, 80

K

kingdom, 7, 44, 72

knowledge, 17, 28, 45, 53

L

life, 3–4, 8–10, 12, 14, 17, 27–28, 30, 52, 54, 64–65, 70–71, 75, 77–78, 80, 85–86
lifestyle, 22, 66
Lord, 19, 32, 44, 51–52, 54, 56–58, 60, 62–63, 69, 71–72, 76–77, 82–83
love, 1, 3, 5–7, 10, 12, 15, 20, 38, 44, 65, 67, 77
lust, 3, 5–6, 65, 70

M

marriage, 1–3, 5, 7–8, 17–19, 27–29, 34, 37, 39, 42–46, 55–58, 61–62, 66–67, 69–70, 72, 74
marriage covenant, 2
minister, 16, 58
ministries, 12–13, 28
mistreatment, 14, 22, 79
money, 12–13, 17, 35, 38, 80

P

pain, 11–12, 17, 19–20, 23, 25, 53, 60
parents, 3, 6, 23

pathway, 27, 77
peace, 39, 80
pearls, 21, 29
permission, 57, 70, 77, 79
plans, 8, 18, 45, 56, 63, 68, 75, 77, 81–83
power, 24, 36, 43, 48
prayer, 11, 48, 51–52, 71–72
praying, 53–54
precious, 21, 29
provider, 25, 86

R

rebellious teens, 8
relationships, 11, 14, 23, 26, 28, 35–36, 45, 53–54, 64, 66, 70, 76, 81–82
responsibility, 24
rubies, 21, 29

S

sex, 12, 38, 69
souls, 5, 8, 66, 68, 77
spiritual attacks, 63
spouse, 7, 35, 37, 41, 47, 56–57, 63
strength, 26, 30–32, 67

sync, 80

T

times, 13, 17, 21, 23–26, 36–38, 43, 45, 47–49, 56, 60, 63, 69–70, 75, 77, 83–85
toilet, 59
transformation, 29
trust, 24, 36–39, 41, 46, 48–49, 53, 55, 60, 63, 77, 80, 83–84
truth, 12, 25, 37, 46, 51, 56, 66–67

U

unconsciousness, 23

V

vainglorious, 6
virtuous, 21, 29
vision, 8, 18, 35, 38, 42–43, 45, 68–69, 71–72
vows, 16, 62

W

wealth, 13, 19

wedding, 10, 17, 34
wisdom, 32, 49, 53

www.ingramcontent.com/pod-product-compliance
Lightning Source LLC
Chambersburg PA
CBHW052201110526
44591CB00012B/2035